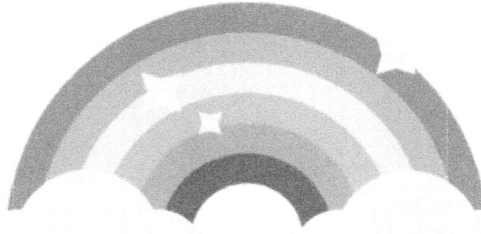

HAPPY EASTER COLORING BOOK

THIS BOOK BELONGS TO

• • • • • • • • • • • • • • • •

Dear Friends,

Inspired by the fairy tale "Magic Paints for the Easter Bunny," this coloring book brings the magic of the story to its pages, allowing children to immerse themselves in the exciting adventures of Eddie the Bunny and bring them to life in vibrant colors. Favorite characters and scenes from the story come alive under the pens of young artists, making the coloring process even more special and magical.

Warmly, Elizabeth Bell.

Made in the USA
Las Vegas, NV
04 March 2024